How a Seed Grows Into a Sunflower

Written by
David Stewart

Illustrated by
Carolyn Franklin

Hold the page up to the light to see the flower opening.

children's press®
An Imprint of Scholastic Inc.
NEW YORK • TORONTO • LONDON • AUCKLAND • SYDNEY
MEXICO CITY • NEW DELHI • HONG KONG
DANBURY, CONNECTICUT

ISBN-13: 978-0-531-20442-9 (lib. bdg.)   978-0-531-20453-5 (pbk.)
ISBN-10: 0-531-20442-1 (lib. bdg.)   0-531-20453-7 (pbk.)

Published in 2008 in the United States
by Children's Press, an imprint of Scholastic Inc.,
557 Broadway, New York, NY 10012.

Copyright © 2008 by
The Salariya Book Company Ltd
25 Marlborough Place, Brighton BN1 1UB, England.
All rights reserved.

A CIP catalog record for this book is available
from the Library of Congress.

Author: **David Stewart** has written many nonfiction books for children on historical topics, including *You Wouldn't Want to be an Egyptian Mummy!* and *You Wouldn't Want to Sail on the Titanic!* He lives in Brighton, England, with his wife and son.

Artist: **Carolyn Franklin** is a graduate of Brighton College of Art, England, specializing in design and illustration. She has worked in animation, advertising, and children's fiction and nonfiction. She has a special interest in natural history and has written many books on the subject, including *Life in the Wetlands* in the WHAT ON EARTH? series and *Egg to Owl* in the CYCLES OF LIFE series.

Consultant: **Monica Hughes** is an experienced Educational Advisor and author of more than one hundred books for young children. She has been headteacher of a primary school, primary advisory teacher and senior lecturer in early childhood education.

Printed and bound in China.
Printed on paper from sustainable sources.

Contents

flower head

petal

bumblebee

What Is a Sunflower?

A sunflower is a plant that lives for only one year. It is very tall, with a long, thick stem. It has a single large, yellow or orange flower head. A sunflower plant needs lots of sun and water to help it grow.

stem

ladybug

stem _____

Plants use energy from the sun to make food.

What Is a Seed?

A sunflower seed contains a tiny new plant and a store of food. The hard outside of the seed is called a **seed coat**. During the cold winter months, the seed lies buried in the ground.

worm

seed coat

In the spring, the warm sun and the rain make the seeds start to grow. This is called **germination**.

seed

Soil contains **minerals**. These are special foods that help the plant to grow.

worm

seed coat splitting

8

What Happens in the Spring?

When the soil warms up in the spring, the hard seed coat splits open. The first root pushes its way out and then grows down into the soil. Soon afterward, a shoot will sprout. The shoot will lift up the seed coat as it grows upward out of the soil.

root

soil

What Do Roots Do?

Small roots now sprout from this first root. They take in minerals and water from the soil to feed the plant. Once the shoot has pushed up through the soil, it grows two tiny green leaves called seed leaves.

ladybug

seed coat

seed leaf

bud

shoot

The store of food inside the seed helps the plant to grow. The bud, hidden between the seed leaves, pushes the seed coat away.

small roots

rain

Why Do Sunflowers Need Rain?

As the young sunflower plant grows taller, more leaves sprout. The leaves use air, rainwater, and energy from sunlight to make food for the plant. This process is called **photosynthesis**.

ladybug

roots

leaf

stem

Flower buds form and the roots grow longer. The roots reach deep down to take water from the soil. They also help to hold the sunflower steady.

garden snail

sunlight

sunlight

How Tall Do Sunflowers Grow?

It takes about 13 weeks for a sunflower to grow fully. Some sunflower plants can grow more than 10 feet tall. The main root can reach 10 feet down below the ground!

Plants can make their own food from the energy in sunlight and from moisture in the air.

ladybug

What Is a Flower Bud?

At the top of the stem is a flower bud. The flower bud follows the sun all day. When the plant is nearly fully grown, the flower bud will open. A flower head is inside the flower bud.

leaf

ladybug

The flower's job is to **reproduce**. It makes new plants that will grow next year.

flower head

flower bud

stem

How Big Is the Flower?

The flower head is larger than a dinner plate. Big yellow petals surround it, making it even bigger. During the day, its petals open up. At night, its petals fold in and close.

flower head

yellow petal

The big, round flower head is made up of lots of tiny flowers. Each tiny flower will become a new sunflower seed.

leaf

tiger moth

bumblebee

Buzzzz
Buzzzz
Buzzzz

19

honey bee

BUZZZZ
buzzzz

pollen sac

pollen grains

Why Do Sunflowers Need Insects?

There is **nectar** inside the sunflower head. Bees and other insects visit the plant to drink the nectar they find there. There is **pollen** on the sunflower head. The bees pick up the sticky pollen grains. As the bees fly from one plant to another, they move the pollen from plant to plant. This is called **pollination**. Sunflowers need pollen to produce new seeds.

Bees need pollen for food. Some bees collect pollen on their hairy bodies. Other bees put it into yellow bags on their legs, called **pollen sacs**.

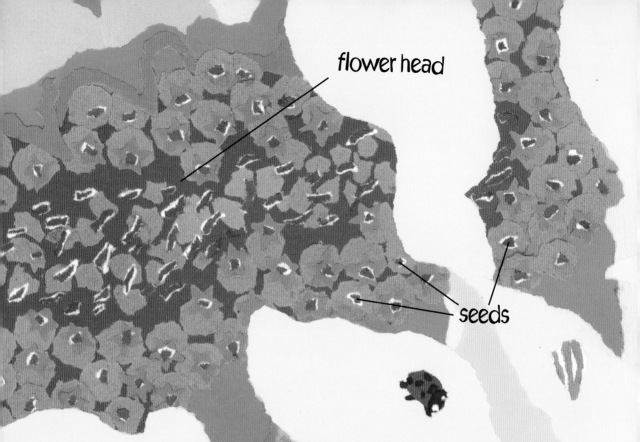

flower head

seeds

How Are Seeds Carried Far Away?

Birds peck at the tiny seeds in the flower head as they ripen. Some seeds are eaten and some are blown away by the wind.

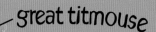

great titmouse

seed ⎯⎯⎯⎯⎯

Seeds on the ground can stick
to the fur of a passing animal.
These seeds may fall off far
away from the main plant.

23

What Happens in the Fall?

In fall the sunflower dies. The seeds that have not been eaten or carried away fall to the ground. Many of the seeds will grow into new sunflower plants in the spring.

ladybug

tree sparrow

seed

The birds eat some of the sunflower seeds. They also scatter some of the seeds so that new plants can grow. This is good for both the birds and the plants.

Sunflower Facts

Sunflower seeds are about 3/8 of an inch long.

A sunflower head can grow to be as wide as 16 inches across.

The main leaves of a sunflower are heart-shaped. They are about 12 inches wide and 8 inches long.

Native Americans grew sunflowers long ago.

Most sunflowers are grown in North and South America, but they also grow in Europe.

Sunflower seeds were brought from America to Spain in 1510.

budding

9 weeks

5 weeks

spring

the seed sprouts leaves

roots

seed

About 200 years ago, farmers started to crush the seeds to make sunflower oil.

The oil is used for cooking. Sunflower seeds are good to eat, too.

The leftovers of the crushed seeds are used to make animal food.

summer

12 weeks

flowering

fully grown

withering

fall

falling seeds

27

Things to Do

Grow Your Own Sunflower

You will need:
One empty yogurt container
Edible sunflower seeds
Popsicle sticks
Pencil
Garden soil

1   Fill the yogurt container
    with soil.

2   Make a hole in the soil
    with your finger (about
    1 in. deep) and drop in
    one seed.

3   Cover the seed with soil.
    Put in a popsicle stick
    with the date written
    on it.

4   Stand the pot in a sunny
    spot and water well. Be
    careful not to let the soil
    get too dry—or too wet.

5   When your plant has at least four leaves, move it carefully into a patch of soil outside.

6   Measure the height of your sunflower every week as it grows.

7   Keep a diary to record how your sunflower is growing.

My Sunflower Diary

Date: 6th   The seed leaves grow.

Date: 7th   The plant is 1 in. tall, and its two leaves are 1/2 in. long.

new seed
ready to
grow

root starts
to grow

birds spread
seeds

shoot starts
to grow

Life Cycle of
a Sunflower

seeds
fall

leaves
appear

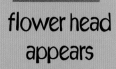

flower head
appears

flower buds
appear

Things to Do

Find Out if a Sunflower Turns Toward the Sun

You will need:
One sunflower plant
 (before the petals
 have opened)
A sunny day
A clock or watch

Record the sun's position at different times of the day.

Note which way your sunflower is facing each time.

Words to Remember

Germination The first stage of growth, when the seed begins to sprout.

Minerals Substances in the soil that help plants grow.

Nectar A sweet juice that plants produce to attract insects.

Photosynthesis The process plants use to make energy from sunlight.

Pollen A powder produced by plants, which the plants use to help make new seeds.

Pollination Moving pollen from one plant to another so that seeds can grow.

Reproduce To make new plants.

Seed leaves The first leaves that are already in the seed when it sprouts.

31

Index